BUSINESS

ETIQUETTE

FOR

MANAGERS

Business Etiquette for Managers

Series " Management Skills for Managers "
By: D.K. Hawkins
Version 1.1 ~January 2022
Published by D.K. Hawkins at KDP
Copyright ©2021 by D.K. Hawkins. All rights reserved.

TABLE OF CONTENTS

INTRODUCTION.

Etiquette is founded on self-respect, respect for others, and being a courteous person consistently, not just occasionally. This entails putting others at ease and making them feel comfortable doing business with you, highlighting the importance of practicing and mastering business etiquette.

Nowadays, an increasing number of people are starting their enterprises, making businesses extremely competitive regardless of the field. As a result, some managers continue to experiment with different marketing tactics to differentiate their products or services from the competition to gain more clients or customers and increase their revenue.

However, it is not all about the product in business. There is a heightened knowledge of what constitutes appropriate corporate activity in today's diminishing global marketplace.

While understanding how to use a fork and knife is an important part of business etiquette, it's equally important to know how to build trust with your customers and clients' customers by bridging the trust gap between your firm and theirs. It has never been more critical for a company to be able to deal with a wide range of individuals and situations than it is now.

It is irrelevant if you are an Internet Marketer or a proprietor of a brick-and-mortar business. The reality is that everyone you contact within your business, whether online or offline, is extremely human and would appreciate being treated as such. As an entrepreneur, it is important to learn to treat people with respect at all times during your discussions and interactions.

It is important to recognize that business etiquette varies by a culture which presents a barrier while conducting business as a global entrepreneur. Today's business is more about your people skills than the quality of your product or service. However, how can you conduct professionally if you do not understand what constitutes appropriate business behavior?

As the proverb says, "you never cease to learn till you die." It is never too late to initiate professional growth to avoid and avoid self-sabotage and embarrassment. You do not need to risk further prospects or status due to a minor blunder.

Just as astronauts master the stars and the fox masters its prey before attacking, you can either master the principles of business etiquette - the science of good business breeding that keeps you in sound business and distinguishes you from your competitors - or you can ignore them and become a "me too" in your industry. The option is yours.

Read on...........................

CHAPTER 1

The Relevance of Business Etiquettes for Managers.

A strong manager's foundation is built on business etiquette. The way you present yourself in a business setting is important to your success in the business world. Your business etiquette is the "first impression" that people remember and sets the tone for how you are seen in a professional context. Appropriate business etiquette will determine how others respond to you as a manager.

Your ties with other businesses are important to your success as a manager. Whether you're communicating with your colleagues or preparing for a business meeting, your business etiquette can help establish the tone for the discussion.

Etiquette is an important part of the job interview process, so it's important to know how to conduct yourself while meeting with a potential employer. If you are the company's manager, correct business etiquette is important to earn your employees' trust and respect.

You may believe that "etiquette" just refers to knowing which fork to pick up first when dining in a fine restaurant. However, "business etiquette" involves much more. It's about body language and eye contact; it's about projecting confidence and making others feel at ease with you, both at networking events and in your job. The following are the essentials of excellent business etiquette.

Maintaining basic decency may appear in plain sense, many people continue to disregard it. The most important guideline of business etiquette is to maintain all child-like courtesies. "Please," "thank you," and "pardon me" are appropriate responses. Apologize when appropriate. Avoid interfering with others. Avoid raising your voice when speaking in person or on the phone. You'll be surprised at how far these fundamentals will take you.

Speak positively about your bosses. Perhaps this is another guideline that harkens back to our elementary school years. It mirrors the adage, "if you have nothing nice to say, say nothing at all."

Occasionally, in an office situation, workers develop camaraderie by criticizing the boss behind his or her back. Take no role in this. You should talk highly about your supervisor both in and out of the office. Making disparaging remarks about him or her reflects poorly on you.

If you're inviting staff to a meeting, make certain you adhere to some fundamental principles. To begin, even if you work in a casual business environment, dress for the meeting in a suit and tie with a secure tie knot.

Having a careless attitude toward your appearance can be offensive to your coworkers. Suiting up enables you to appear prepared, authoritative, and as though you respect your colleagues' time. Before the meeting, write an email outlining the purpose, the anticipated duration, and the topics to be addressed.

Maintain eye contact throughout the meeting and express gratitude to attendees for their time and involvement. Employees often leave meetings wondering if their efforts were even appreciated, which is why this appreciation is important. Also, perhaps most crucially, switch off your cell phone during meetings.

Also, observe proper email etiquette. Even if the message is harsh, you should always begin an email with a polite, welcoming line such as "I appreciate your." or "thank you for." Emails should be concise.

Avoid using all caps (which conveys a sense of yelling) or uncommon colors that can be difficult to read.

Always begin with a salutation and conclude with a phrase such as "regards" or "best." These are polished and pleasant without being excessively sentimental. Include a subject line relevant to the email's subject; avoid confusing subjects like "for you" or "a query."

Take note of your body language. Pay attention to your body language; smile and maintain a straight posture. According to Albert Mehrabian, a UCLA psychology professor, 55% of the message you send at any given time is through your visual appearance.

You do not need to extend your hand first when shaking hands. Gender equality has been achieved in business. When conversing with a coworker in person, maintain a distance of approximately 3 feet. This is close enough to avoid yelling but not so close that you intrude on his or her personal space.

Avoid the most common awkwardness traps. Everyone has encountered an unpleasant situation in which they cannot recall the name of someone they met at a networking event. Allow yourself to be fooled by this.

Simply grin and say, "My mind has gone blank; could you please tell me your name?" Alternatively, "I recognize your face but have forgotten your name." Following that, make a concerted attempt to recall the individual's name!

CHAPTER 2

Effective Business Etiquettes For Managers At Conferences.

Another area of concern for most managers is business etiquette. You may be unable to interact with clients while on the road. However, once you've attended your first meeting or set loot in a conference hall, you're in a business setting, and etiquette concerns arise.

It's especially difficult to balance an acceptable business response with a polite one. Neither is mutually exclusive. However, many managers have not encountered these etiquette issues at home because the circumstance presents itself for the first time while abroad.

Regardless of whether this is your first time at an industry conference, the opportunity to meet and network with other professionals in your field is unrivaled. Other members of your firm, possibly even your supervisor, may attend in some instances. You are representing your firm and should conduct yourself professionally in any situation.

There will be specific difficulties to overcome, such as introducing yourself to strangers and attending evening activities while still obtaining enough sleep to prepare for the following day's seminars.

You may notice that some people are more assertive and pushy at a conference. Maintain your composure and keep in mind that the setting's intensity and proximity might bring out the worst in individuals. Then allow it to bring out your best qualities. Face the struggle because the rewards for your career are well worth it.

Consume alcohol in moderation.

After years of conference attendance, I believe I've seen it all—some female managers who have consumed an excessive amount of alcohol dance on tables. Men passionately kiss ladies (who are not their wives) in public because both of them have had too much to drink.

At a conference, it appears as though attendees want to let their hair down. While fun and games may be engaging in the time, a minute-by-minute recounting of different sophomoric behaviors cannot be comfortable for participants upon their return to work.

The simplest method to minimize the possibility of humiliating behavior is to limit alcohol consumption. This may seem obvious, but many first-time conference-goers overlook this mandate when the drinks are complimentary. Before you enter the first conference event, make a promise to yourself that you will have no more than one drink.

After a glass of wine or martini, switch to soda water. Limit your crazy nights and excessive consumption to non-business situations, such as when you're with your loving family or understanding friends, not while your job or future career moves are at stake. Even if no one from your office attends, news spreads and could come back to haunt you.

Now that you've resolved the primary conference issue, there are a few other points to consider to make your conference experience easier.

Appropriate attire.

This is not the moment to bust out that sultry gown you've been saving to wear to work or to slip into those flattering but lethal high-heel pumps. After a day of standing, your feet will welcome the low-heeled shoes!

Suit up in elegant pantsuits or skirted suits and adhere to the conference's dress code. Instead of a backless dress or a slit-to-high-thigh skirt, make a fashion statement with a designer scarf or distinctive jewelry. (From a practical standpoint, dress in layers. Conference halls are known for being extremely cold or extremely hot.)

Smiling and handshake.

Maintain a cheerful disposition. You'll feel more at ease and in a better mood, and people will respond with warmth and friendliness. Remember to smile and extend your hand whenever you are introduced, or someone approaches you with a question. Conferences provide a golden opportunity to network and meet new people—and a grin and a quick handshake make the process go more smoothly.

Repetition is a memory assist, linking that person's name with another person with the same name you already know. Since some males have been instructed not to extend their hands first to women, you must extend your hand for the handshake. To assist you in recalling a person's name later, repeat it loudly as you shake hands.

Be punctual.

Attending panels and other events on time can be difficult because of the strange surroundings and distractions, but don't allow this to deter you from making it on time for your meal or finding a restroom.

When doors are often opening and closing due to latecomers to a conference, it disturbs the remaining attendees. Also, the mouse may obstruct the speaker. It's possible for a woman arrived late because she was flaky or was still doing her cosmetics.

Contrary to popular belief, refrain from reinforcing that image: Be kind and punctual. Allow plenty of time for your commute, even if it means arriving early. You can always bring a book or a project to work on.

Maintain business cards.

This is a massive opportunity to network with individuals in your business. Bring plenty of business cards and keep them with you on all occasions. When people see their names in print, they recall them. Also, the cards you gather may turn out to be from important business contacts later on.

When meeting new people, initiate as many business card exchanges as feasible. Make a note on the back of each card you receive so you can recall the contact later while you're sorting through a deck of cards following the trip.

Participate in a group.

It can be rather frightening to go into a room full of strangers and realize you don't know anyone. There is a corporate responsibility to network and meet people at an opening event mixer. However, women have been taught to await introductions. This case is an exception to the conventional rule, and getting started will require some fortitude.

To begin, remind yourself that you are a brilliant, fascinating, and professional individual whom others are eager to meet. Look around the room for a small group that isn't squished together in an exclusive huddle. Approach, smile, and say, "How are you? You appear to be engaged in an engaging conversation. I hope it's okay if I join you. My given name is"

Alternatively, you may come across someone standing alone, possibly taking in the view the same way you are. If there is amusement, you may approach, smile, and say, "How are you? Don't you think this band is quite good?

My given name is "and reach out your hand. Alternatively, you can comment on the unique presentation of the food or mention that you saw the person earlier in the day at a seminar as a way to initiate a conversation.

Often, these meetings are intended to encourage participants to mingle and meet new people. For instance, there may be an "ice-breaker," such as instructions on the backs of name tags directing participants to seek out specific individuals.

Alternatively, you may be assigned to a specific table or group. These devices should assist you in initiating contact. Simply ensure that the conversation continues after your initial greetings.

Making appropriate small conversation.

Once you've initiated the conversation, it may be challenging to maintain it. After you've addressed the standard inquiries about someone's profession and the seminars he or she has attended, it may be challenging to think of anything more to say. After all, those individuals are strangers to you.

To begin, be cautious and adhere to the conventional principles of small chat - avoid discussing money, religion, or politics. Your industry is an obvious choice. Perhaps you might bring up some recent developments, current events, or even general problems. Simple non-work conversation starters include movies, vacations, music, art, sports, the weather, or books.

You may learn a lot about a person simply by looking at their areas of interest. While some individuals enjoy discussing their children, they should allow someone else to initiate the topic and engage cautiously. If you must discuss your job or employer, keep a good attitude. You do not want to disparage your business or act as a complainant in a public forum.

Avoid dominating the conversation, but also avoid being a shrinking violet. Asking questions or others is among the most effective methods to keep a conversation going. Most people enjoy discussing themselves, and it will help them feel more at ease. It's also a great idea to be familiar with airport customs regulations.

CHAPTER 3

Business Etiquette Facilitates Repeat Business And Long-Term Business Friendships.

Many managers are so focused on profit margins that they overlook that among the most effective methods to boost the bottom line is to just "be kind." Even though much commerce is conducted via technology, proper face-to-face, and online etiquette is important. Due to the changing business style in the twenty-first century, what is proper and acceptable is not always obvious.

Naturally, when in doubt, the important point is to remember to say and do things that make others feel good about being in your space and doing business with you. This enables you to cultivate relationships that result in referrals, repeat business, and long-term business friendships. The following are some helpful hints:

1. Send handwritten notes of appreciation. Allow technology to keep you from losing your unique touch.

A handwritten note communicates the extremely powerful message that you regard the individual you are working with.

There are occasions when an email "thank you" is appropriate; for example, if you have been engaging with the customer/client primarily via email, continue to do so; however, if the meeting included a face-to-face interaction that demands a thank you, take the time to write a note. People retain handwritten notes for a considerably longer period than they do emails.

While an email can be stored, many recipients will read the thank you and delete the email. In an age when so few are sent, sending a handwritten note distinguishes you from your competition and demonstrates that you are a class act.

2. Return all phone calls or respond to all messages. It is natural to reject phone calls from salespeople or business contacts you do not wish to speak; nevertheless, this is not sensible. How you manage every day phone calls reveals how you operate your business, respect your clients, and feel about people in general.

There will be telephone calls that you do not wish to answer, but no one ever said business was simple. Endeavor to return all phone calls or request that your assistant do so with deference if you do not wish to purchase what they are selling, express gratitude for the offer, and politely decline. Depending on the nature of your goods, you may occasionally overlook a potential consumer.

If they are in sales, you may be overlooking someone who can introduce you to a large number of people or provide you with the referrals you seek. Because business is all about connections, keep in mind that the person whose call you are ignoring may be the one with whom you wish to speak for the reason that benefits both your firm and your customers.

3. Demonstrate an interest in people. When you meet someone in business for the first time, avoid immediately pitching them your goods.

Yes, you may be passionate about your product, and it may be the best invention since man found fire, but people are uninterested in what you're selling until you demonstrate that you care about them. Selling a product without first getting to know the person you're attempting to sell to sends a clear message that you're solely interested in the transaction and couldn't care less about the person.

Strive to become acquainted with the individual you meet for the first time. Learn about their needs and determine whether you can genuinely assist them, then follow up and give your solution to their needs, hopefully, your product.

4. Acquaint yourself with names and faces. When you meet someone in business for the first time,

learn their name and show enough interest in them to remember it. Make it a point to remember the names of everybody you meet, even if you have to ask them to repeat it for you.

A wonderful approach to remembering someone's name when meeting them for the first time is to repeat it often throughout your interaction with them. That requires you to be more interested in learning about others than discussing yourself. Learning about others will enhance your memory and is simply more appropriate.

5. Be aware of who is in front of you. If you have someone in your office, direct your gaze away from your computer screen and toward them. If you think highly enough of someone to make an appointment, then respect both their and your time. When it may be difficult to avoid distractions such as emails, text messages and phone calls, the best action is to silence everything while in a meeting.

6. Distribute a single business card. Always hand out one business card and never offer someone a

handful of your cards in exchange for a reference. When you meet with them, focus on leaving a lasting impression, present one business card professionally, and express your appreciation for recommendations. They will understand. Also, if you make a favorable impression, they will gladly refer you to business.

7. Make every effort to follow through. Maintaining your word in business might assist you in establishing a reputation for unwavering integrity. That will entice others to do business with you, and strong integrity is among the most effective branding concepts you can use to describe your business.

When you commit to business, try your best to keep it. If you RSV'P for an event, it is important that you attend or contact the next day to apologize.

Simply follow through on a promise to return a phone call. If you produce a bill or commit to doing business with someone, keep your word. Maintain booked appointments or call to reschedule as soon as possible. Following through demonstrates that you are the business professional you claim to be.

8. Never send out self-disclosing mass emails. If you're sending the same email to many people in business, respect their email privacy by doing a "blind courtesy copy" that hides everyone else's email address.

9. Do not SMS the daily special. If an individual has not requested your business texts or has no contact with the individual, do not send a text message requesting business. Even if you have the best bargain available, you must respect other people's right to solitude and tranquillity.

Proper business etiquette will assist you in developing long-term, high-quality relationships, and business will come your way even when you are not expecting it. Treating others in business the way you want to be treated can ensure your firm achieves the success and profitability you desire. Prioritizing people over money will ensure your business's viability for years to come.

CHAPTER 4

Business Etiquette - Cell Phone and Texting Do's and Don'ts.

In this technological age of rapid and continuous connectivity, an increasing number of people are wearing their cell phones as permanent appendages! If they are not wearing it in their ear through Bluetooth or a hand-held gadget, they are busily texting with their heads buried in their phones.

Oprah Winfrey has launched a national campaign to end texting while driving, and when Oprah talks, the rest of the world listens. Not only is it dangerous to chat or text while driving for the reasons outlined in her program and accident reports but misusing communication devices conveys the wrong message in a business situation.

Here is some common sense but often overlooked phone and texting business etiquette tips for managers:

Always turn off your phone's ringer when you're in meetings, restaurants, or other public areas or when you're with others. Your immediate surroundings should be the focus of your attention.

Refuse to take or make calls at a restaurant table. It is simply impolite to be rude to those with you and those in your immediate vicinity. If you absolutely must accept the call, relocate to a place where you will not annoy anyone. If there is no other secluded area, proceed outside.

Placing your phone in a briefcase, handbag, or pocket is a good idea. Don't lay it on the table. The vibration sound will be distracting to others, and you will not be able to resist looking at it from time to time.

Avoid checking for messages and texting when in the same situation. It should be for a compelling reason: an emergency, an important customer issue, etc. If you expect to hear from someone about an urgent concern, let the others know that you must check periodically and apologize for the distraction.

When you make (or receive) a call, keep an eye on the volume of your voice. Nobody else wants to hear your talk, and having to listen to it because your voice is too loud is distracting and disturbing. Before resuming your call, exit the area.

Avoid raising your voice. Simply because you cannot hear the other person does not mean they cannot hear you! If you have difficulty hearing the chat, move to a location with stronger reception.

While on the phone or texting, keep an eye on your surroundings. You may put yourself in danger if you are unaware of what is happening. You may have alienated one group and offended another - even put yourself in danger.

Thus, you can walk while chewing gum! That is not to say that you should walk while conversing or texting. When your mind is focused on the discussion or message, you may accidentally bump into other people or items, trip, fall, or walk into oncoming traffic.

The fundamental reason to practice excellent and safe cell phone and texting practices is regard, consideration, and respect for others. Because others will judge you based on your actions, displaying proper etiquette standards will elevate your status in their eyes.

Consider the facial expressions of those irritated by cell phone users – they are often ones of disgust or displeasure. You demonstrate behavior that communicates to others that you are not as important as the individual I am communicating with! When you text with your head buried in your phone, you are oblivious to the people around you.

Texting or using your cell phone as a mode of communication is a convenient way to communicate. You may be oblivious to the wrong message you send to others around you by failing to practice proper business and social manners.

CHAPTER 5

Business Etiquette – Table Manners.

In today's world, business is conducted outside the four walls of your company's headquarters. Business negotiations and transactions occur at golf courses, entertainment events, social places, and restaurants.

There are many forces at work to develop corporate relationships, partnerships, and collaborations. We recommend mastering the proper etiquette for productive and pleasant business encounters to navigate difficult situations with grace and diplomacy.

The following are five valuable pointers for proper business dining etiquette:

How the Clock Works.

If you have a business breakfast, lunch, or dinner booking, it is important to arrive early. Arriving early is a modest act of civility and decorum. By arriving early, you can use the restroom, check your messages, power off your electronics and minimize distractions during the business dinner. By not arriving late, you are essentially respecting everyone's time.

Deja-Vu.

If you have already selected the day, location, and time of your business event, we recommend that you visit the restaurant's website to examine the menu and obtain instructions. By previewing the menu, you will have sufficient time to choose what to eat.

You can even choose one or two meals if they are not available in the order you want. This is highly advantageous on the day of the business event, as you can make a more informed choice about your meal without wasting time or delaying the order status for the entire table.

Beer Bottles.

You should decide whether or not to order alcohol before the business meal. You can check with the event's host, other attendees, or your supervisor to determine whether ordering wine, a cocktail, beer, or other alcoholic beverages is acceptable.

Also, if you decide to order alcohol, take in mind the client or the nature of the business meal. If this is your first meeting, we strongly advise you to abstain from drinking. If you feel at ease with your business counterparts and maintain positive business relationships, buying alcohol may not be a bad idea. Ascertain your tolerance level and drink wisely.

Speaking the Truth.

Before the business gathering, spend some time brainstorming possible subjects for discussion during the dinner. This would be an opportunity to refresh your knowledge of current events, sports, business trends, entertainment, travel, and technology, among other things.

Also, you can visit the websites of your business opponents to learn about their business culture, objectives, missions, and current national or worldwide projects. Avoid contentious themes that may not be acceptable for a business discussion.

Always bring more cash with you while attending business events such as these. While you may not be paying for the dinner, you may be required to pay cash for transportation, parking, valet, or other post-business event activities.

Depending on the business event location, ATMs may be challenging to locate or cumbersome to use. Also, not every restaurant/venue accepts credit cards or personal/business cheques.

CHAPTER 6

Business Etiquette: Should You Give A Handshake Or A Hug?

Generally, business begins and concludes with a handshake. It is prevalent in a wide variety of civilizations. It both greets and farewells. It is a secure web-to-web link that utilizes two to three pumps. It bestows love and goodwill, which is beneficial for business.

Not everyone enjoys physical interaction. A handshake is an appropriate technique to extend an invitation and establish contact without invading another's personal space.

What do you plan to do if you encounter a hugger?

To hug or not to hug, that is the question.

Do you enjoy hugging people?

Have you ever given or on the receiving end of an awkward hug?

Kisses on both cheeks are reserved for close friends in French culture. In different regions of American culture, particularly the southern states, a short hug is often exchanged. Similar to the European double cheek kiss, these embraces are typically reserved for close friends or long-standing associates but may occur without permission or request.

What if, as you prepare to leave a business meeting abruptly, your former colleague reaches out to offer you a short hug? That, indeed, has occurred to me. Yes, someone with whom I had worked for years came out to hug me. I stared at my client after the embrace and hugged him.

Also, two additional colleagues, neither of whom I knew well. I was imprisoned.

What should I do?

Do I extend a handshake and give them the impression that I'm not interested in hugging them?

Alternatively, do I go ahead and extend a hug to avoid offending someone's feelings?

Hugging is a highly individual option that changes from person to person. Our individual family history, culture, and environment contribute significantly to our acceptance or disapproval of a hug. Hugging and even kissing are considered acceptable in different cultures.

If you know two people well and others you do not know well at the party, you can begin the hello or goodbye process with those you do not know well first. You have demonstrated that you appreciate their presence and space by extending your hand in preparation for a good handshake. After that, you can turn to your pals and hug them. This way, nobody feels uneasy.

What if someone reaches out to hug you and you are unfamiliar with them?

Take the initiative and initiate a handshake when someone approaches you for a hug. Extend your hand toward them and address them directly. Assure that your feet are securely planted to avoid shaking your hand and pulling you in for the embrace. Body language is a highly effective communicator, and these gestures should assist the non-hugger in avoiding unwanted embraces.

Etiquette is mainly concerned with how you make people feel. It is a style of being with others that fosters comfort. Our objective is to establish rapport and establish a relationship with others. We must be conscious of our surroundings.

As with any issue, it is always prudent to take a more conservative stance. The bottom line is to be aware of your clients' needs and respect their boundaries regarding professional hugs.

CHAPTER 7

Business Etiquette - How to Provide Excellent Customer Service.

Competitors have no chance when the objective is to restore the word "service" to customer service.

Here's how to get there:

Seek Out Smiling Faces.

While quality assistance may be challenging to come by, it should not come at the expense of creating a great business image. Anyone who represents a business should project a positive attitude. The first encounter in person or over the phone has the power to break or make an impression.

Psychologists agree that even over the telephone, a smile can be "heard." When customers encounter a sour countenance or a harsh tone, they may become hesitant to conduct business with the business.

Construct Relationships.

Outstanding customer service professionals understand how to convert infrequent consumers into committed ones. It all begins with the extension of basic courtesies to everyone. If a customer initiates a casual discussion, be mindful of proper etiquette. Personal grievances or lengthy tales are not acceptable. Keeping a pleasant business demeanor without appearing aloof demonstrates professionalism.

The most effective relationship-building tactics that leave a lasting impression are remembering a customer's name and addressing them personally upon return. Recall their preferred product and devise a method for utilizing that information.

You may establish yourself as a useful resource by providing professional advice or sharing product expertise. These are the principles that underpin long-term business relationships.

Compensate For Loyalty.

When incentives are presented, returning consumers will understand how valued they are. Implement a perks-based rewards program to keep customers pleased and coming back. There are many methods to express gratitude and make regular clients feel special.

Offering unique product samples or invitations to private sales are effective methods to demonstrate gratitude. The only constraints on the ideas are a limited budget and the capacity for creativity.

Exceed Expectations.

Whenever feasible, strive to exceed customer expectations. Everyone yearns to receive what they pay for in any commercial transaction. However, when a business gives "extraordinary" service, customers reciprocate with repeat business and favorable word-of-mouth promotion.

This additional service might be as simple as delivering products to a car or as extravagant as offering free shipment on occasion. The surprise of "a little something extra"—such as the 13th item in a dozen—is always gratefully welcomed.

Request Feedbacks.

Allowing customers to voice problems or offer suggestions is an important component of providing outstanding customer service. Many businesses now hire marketing research agencies to monitor the quality of their goods and services. When clients take the time to submit feedback, it should be treated positively and as a chance to improve.

Customer complaints should be investigated. Quickly and effectively resolving issues can convert a dissatisfied complainant into a satisfied customer. Obtaining a satisfying resolution or adhering to a call-back promise are sometimes ignored measures. As a result, the customer is not just unhappy but also frustrated.

Abandon The Rules.

Few phrases irritate customers more than hearing the classic "It is not our policy" speech. These words nearly always result in a lost consumer. While policies and processes are crucial for running a successful organization, every rule has an exception.

Astute managers understand when to make those exceptions. When the cost of deviating from the policy is carefully weighed against the customer's future spending capacity, the conclusion is generally apparent.

The Customer Is Always Right.

Even when they are incorrect, a consumer is always correct. This message appears to have gotten lost somewhere along the line in the best practices guidebook. No consumer has ever been won over through correction, contempt, argument, or taking for granted. If a customer chooses not to do business with a business, it should never be for any of the reasons mentioned above.

CHAPTER 8

Business Etiquette – Communication.

Maintaining Eye Contact.

While eye contact is important in the United States, it can be somewhat problematic in certain nations throughout the world due to the likelihood of an unintentional misreading of the other person.

Voice.

Maintain a grin in your voice while communicating. Your tone of voice conveys your attitude.

Smile.

The most important item to wear!

Listening.

Listening is the most important talent, yet it is also the most challenging. Concentrate on the other person's words rather than what you say next. You are not required to fill in any of a conversation's quiet pauses. Even if you disagree with anything, listen and nod to demonstrate that you are considering the other person's point of view and certainly avoid interfering, particularly with a complaint, which is often little more than a need for an outlet or a listening ear.

Barriers.

Eliminate any boundaries between you and the person with whom you are conversing. This also reduces the space between you and demonstrates that you are receptive to what the other person says. Speaking over your eyeglasses is a strict no-no.

Networking.

High and to the right, name badges are worn. If necessary, use the buddy system to introduce each other to someone. You are not required to rush through your talk as you circulate. Have fun and avoid running through your thoughts.

After introducing yourself, summarize your company's mission in a single statement. If necessary, request business cards and place theirs in your left pocket while keeping your own in your right.

Telephone.

Phone call screening is not as straightforward as it appears. First, introduce yourself and your company before talking with the individual. While speaking, stand up and smile. Individuals can detect this over the phone in some way. Your calls will be screened solely for identification, not for the goal of removal.

Naturally, when you're on the phone, your focus should be on that and not on paperwork or your computer. Avoid chit-chatting and other unprofessional behavior to maintain your professional image. Also, always have a message ready and wait if you receive someone's voice mail.

Notes of Appreciation.

They're always suitable, whether handwritten or typed, even though they appear to be far less prevalent than they should be. Also, if you have an interview, you must follow up with a thank-you note.

CHAPTER 9

The Fundamental Rules of Appropriate Business Meeting Etiquette.

Individual behavior, both professionally and personally, reveals a lot about who you are as a person. Generally, common sense informs us what constitutes appropriate behavior and what does not, particularly when in a business meeting.

Your professional manner or lack thereof can make or break a business deal and how clients, supervisors, and coworkers approach you in the workplace. That is why you must adhere to sound business etiquette when attending meetings of any kind.

The first and most fundamental rule of appropriate etiquette is to always be on time for meetings.

If possible, arrive a few minutes early. This communicates to the other attendees that you are invested in the meeting and attentive by arriving early. Be courteous and shake the host's hand to express your gratitude for inviting you to join.

The second fundamental rule is always being prepared and having everything in order before the meeting.

It's a good idea to know the purpose of the meeting and conduct some study on the subject in advance, so you'll know what's likely to be addressed. Bring any supporting documents and other information that will enable you to contribute significantly to the meeting.

By being prepared and conducting a study on the subject before the meeting, you will advise your manager and coworkers more effectively and ask and answer pertinent questions. By arriving at the meeting prepared, you demonstrate to your employer, clients, and coworkers that you are organized and focused.

The third fundamental element of excellent etiquette is to be kind and attentive during your encounter.

Never speak out of turn, be anxious to get your point across, or speak over those attempting to express a different argument. Do not engage in any other activity during the meeting while another person is speaking, as this demonstrates a lack of attention and respect for the other person.

If you are hosting the meeting, you should be properly prepared and notify all participants in advance of the meeting's date, time, and place. Send e-mail invitations and office notes in advance to give your coworkers time to prepare.

Also, you should educate your coworkers about the upcoming meeting's subjects and offer them a clear plan. Your meeting should have a set start and end time to allow for a more effective discussion of agenda items.

Maintain control of the meeting's progress by staying on track and concentrating on the important points. If you have presenters or guest speakers, you should inquire about their time for their presentations and plan accordingly. This will ensure that the meeting proceeds smoothly and that there is no time lag between subjects.

Above all, maintain a diplomatic demeanor, calm demeanor, and avoid confrontations. As the meeting draws close, recap the themes discussed and conclude.

If a follow-up meeting is necessary, advise the attendees to notify them of the date, time, and location. Always keep in mind that correct business etiquette is important to the success of your professional career, so always put your best foot forward and mind your manners.

CHAPTER 10

Business Cards Etiquette.

Among the most fundamental requirements for earning the respect of others is to practice excellent business etiquette. We all desire to associate with cultured individuals, and etiquette is an important component of culture.

Understanding business etiquette enables you to communicate comfortably with your customers and business associates and quickly establish a positive rapport. While the subject of business etiquette is extensive and beyond the scope of this essay, we can undoubtedly cover one very common but important etiquette issue that business people often face: exchanging business cards.

In most of the globe, business cards are used to exchange or obtain contact information and other important personal details about business acquaintances.

However, much depends on how the business card is handed over or how the receiver receives the business card. Certain countries have established a standard for receiving and giving business cards, but the global etiquettes for business card exchange can be summarized in the following principles.

a) Always get your business cards produced on superior material and professional graphics. A business card is more than a piece of paper with your contact information; it is a tool for branding your firm.

b) Business cards are a widely accepted method of presenting necessary personal information to business contacts. When attending a business meeting or social event, ensure that you have a sufficient amount of business cards.

c) Attempt to exchange business cards at the start or conclusion of the meeting.

d) Make a habit of studying and commenting on business cards whenever you receive one. This demonstrates that you regard the one who presents the card with due regard. If you have any reservations, always resolve them before storing them.

e) If you're traveling to a foreign country where English is not the predominant business language, it's a good idea to have the rear of your business card written in your native tongue. Also, while giving out a business card to someone, it is required that you place the part with the foreign language version on top.

f) Avoid thrusting your business card at strangers. Business cards are exchanged only after both parties demonstrate an interest in communicating.

g) While it is acceptable to include a tagline or mention your business's unique selling proposition on your business card, avoid turning it into a bit of billboard in the process.

Apart from these fundamental business card exchange etiquette guidelines, certain countries have politeness guidelines. China and Japan are home to two particularly exceptional examples.

When handing out business cards in China, it is polite to hold them in both hands and never write on the back of another person's card unless encouraged to do so. It is usual in China to have your title on your business card, and it is preferable to have one side printed in Chinese with golden lettering, as gold is considered a fortunate hue.

Japan's accepted business card exchange laws are slightly different than those in China. Business cards are always accepted in two hands here but can be offered in one. Business cards are treated the same way as real people are. Business cards should include the individual's title, as Japan's status and hierarchy are heavily emphasized.

Business cards are an essential component of any company's marketing strategy. If you know how to maximize the value of your business cards, you can be confident that they will pay for themselves many times over.

CHAPTER 11

Business Etiquette Rules That Are Often Broken.

Business etiquette is described as "the established standard of courteous behavior in society or among members of a certain profession or group." Many individuals associate etiquette with "prim and proper." However, it is about respect rather than a formality in business, not to mention that it directly impacts the bottom line.

Continue reading to see whether you (or someone you work with) could benefit from some work etiquette development.

Rule 1.

You are perpetually late for meetings - including your own. You are extremely significant, and the world needs to know it. The mere fact that you attend a meeting at all is sufficient and, to ensure that your presence is felt, you often seek a repeat of what you missed.

How do you correct it? Easy. Be punctual, if not a minute or two early. If you conduct meetings on your own, avoid waiting for everyone to arrive and recapitulating what was discussed. If individuals are perpetually late due to missing important information, they will eventually learn to arrive on time.

Another trick is to set a new trend by scheduling 50-minute meetings rather than hour-long ones. This allows everyone enough time to move from one meeting to the next, including a restroom break if necessary!

Rule 2.

Your meetings are often running late due to the gravity of the subject at hand. If attendees have other commitments or tasks to complete, you are irrelevant.

How do you correct it? Utilize the timer! More essential, keep your meetings productive and focused. Often, only around three topics may be successfully discussed without feedback in an hour (unless it is a lecture). Establish a time limit for each topic and adjourn or reschedule the meeting when the time limit expires.

Rule 3.

You always answer your phone, even when someone is speaking to you. This appears to be especially important to do when the other person has come to your office and has been attempting to discuss something that appears to be essential to them but is irrelevant to you.

How do you correct it? If you have an appointment, simply do not answer the phone! If you absolutely must, explain to the other person that you expect a call you would prefer not to miss and request permission to answer. The other person should be able to approve or decline the request, regardless of their status in the organization.

Rule 4.

Along with answering your business phone, you use your mobile phone to react to emails and text messages during meetings. You are a highly busy person, and everything you do must be taken care of immediately.

How do you correct it? You are aware of the answer. Maintain a vibrating phone and avoid checking it every two minutes. Reschedule the meeting if there is an urgent matter that can't wait until its end. If the meeting is long enough, a "technology" break every 20 minutes might be a good choice. Email responses can take up to 20 minutes, based on my personal experience.

Rule 5.

You enjoy barging into other people's desks unannounced, occasionally while they are on the phone or focusing intensely on something. You proceed to check your email and text messages and converse about non-work-related topics.

How do you correct it? Take a walk and rest on your own or quietly check before entering. If you truly have a business to discuss, call/email in advance, "knock" on the cube, or inquire, "Is this a good time?" before barging in. If others are breaching the rule, rise to give the appearance that you are going somewhere. Then, if it is genuinely a business visit, schedule the "visit."

Rule 6.

Because you are so vital and busy, you believe in informing others that you will be working till midnight. Also, if you are the boss, your staff should be aware of this and should be checking their email regularly.

Boundaries are essential for work/life balance, and failing to maintain them reflects adversely on how others see you and your lifestyle. How do you correct it? Send the email in the morning! Alternatively, unless the employee needs to be "on-call," tell this to him/her in advance. This is a significant issue for most people, and we shall discuss it further in another issue.

Rule7.

Because you want everyone to hear you, you prefer to speak all the time loudly. It is what it is and irrelevant if others become preoccupied around you.

How do you correct it? It's possible that your voice is naturally a little loud - or that you're deaf. However, if your voice is excessively loud, close your door while on the phone or conversing with someone. If you work in a cubicle, post a notice beside your phone that reads, "Please use your internal voice." If you're calling someone, they're not going to like it when you yell in their ear.

These are recurrent and straightforward practices that show disrespect and rudeness in the workplace, and they are specific to correct, in my opinion. The United States has a massive problem regarding employees being actively and positively connected with each other and their jobs.

It can affect you and your business's bottom line from productivity and work environment. Respecting others' time, appreciating what they do, and setting a positive example will enhance workplace productivity and engagement.

Distribute this material to members of your organization, your human resources department, and anybody else you believe could benefit from it. Create a seminar. Create some guidelines for new hires.

At the absolute least, do what is best for your success and the company's bottom line.

CONCLUSION.

With the guts to start your own business or manage another's, it is always prudent to give your all. When you show yourself professionally, the current clients will become lasting customers who refer your services to others.

Making a favorable impression in business is important to success. When you're about to meet new people or conduct business networking, how you present yourself is often a reflection of your competence in the eyes of both coworkers and supervisors. As you learned as a child, there are some "golden rules" to follow in personal and professional life. Here are the top ten guidelines of business etiquette to remember.

While business etiquette is often overlooked, it is important. Respect and honor are even more important for entrepreneurs looking to start their businesses. By demonstrating your ability to be punctual, use acceptable language and express gratitude, you will establish a firm foothold in the corporate world.

While financing and promoting a business might be challenging, maintaining proper etiquette should be a natural and effortless approach to attract consumers and keep personnel.

It is important to incorporate business etiquette into your business and marketing efforts. Correct business etiquette can help ensure your organization's long-term growth and profitability.

Thanks for Reading.

Management Skills for Managers

1.   Time Management for Managers

2.   Employee Coaching for Managers

3.   Team Building for Managers

4.   Self Confidence for Managers

5.   Negotiation Skills for Managers

6.   Customer Service Skills for Managers

7.   Assertiveness for Managers

8.   Business Etiquette for Managers

9.   Listening Skills for Managers

10   Leadership Skills for Managers

11.   Communication Skills for Managers

12.   Presentation Skills for Managers

13.   Stress Management for Managers

14.   Decision Making for Managers

15.   Conflict Management for Managers

Author Bio

D.K. Hawkins. D.K. enjoys reading personal business books as well as spending time outdoors. More books will come in this collection, so please follow on Amazon for more books.

Thank you for your purchase of this book.

I honestly do appreciate it and appreciate you, my excellent customer.

God Bless You.

D.K. Hawkins.

Made in the USA
Monee, IL
24 April 2022

95335851R00046